Caught by the Sea

MY LIFE ON BOATS

33

D0034637

Also by Gary Paulsen

Alida's Song

The Beet Fields

The Boy Who Owned the School

The Brian Books: *The River, Brian's Winter* and *Brian's Return*

Canyons

The Car

The Cookcamp

The Crossing

Dogsong

Father Water, Mother Woods

The Glass Café

Guts

Harris and Me

Hatchet

The Haymeadow

How Angel Peterson Got His Name

The Island

The Monument

My Life in Dog Years

Nightjohn

The Night the White Deer Died

Puppies, Dogs, and Blue Northers

The Rifle

Sarny: A Life Remembered

The Schernoff Discoveries

Soldier's Heart

The Transall Saga

Tucket's Travels (The Tucket's West series, Books One through Five)

The Voyage of the Frog

The White Fox Chronicles

The Winter Room

Picture books, illustrated by Ruth Wright Paulsen:

Canoe Days and *Dogteam*

GARY PAULSEN

Caught
by the
SEA

MY LIFE ON BOATS

LAUREL-LEAF
BOOKS

For Rick Schrock,
who knows the wind

Published by
Dell Laurel-Leaf
an imprint of
Random House Children's Books
a division of Random House, Inc.
New York

Copyright © 2001 by Gary Paulsen
Maps by James Sinclair

Visit us on the Web! www.randomhouse.com/teens

Educators and librarians, for a variety of teaching tools, visit us at
www.randomhouse.com/teachers

ISBN: 0-440-40716-8

RL: 6.4

Reprinted by arrangement with Delacorte Press

Printed in the United States of America

September 2003

10 9 8 7 6 5 4 3 2 1

OPM

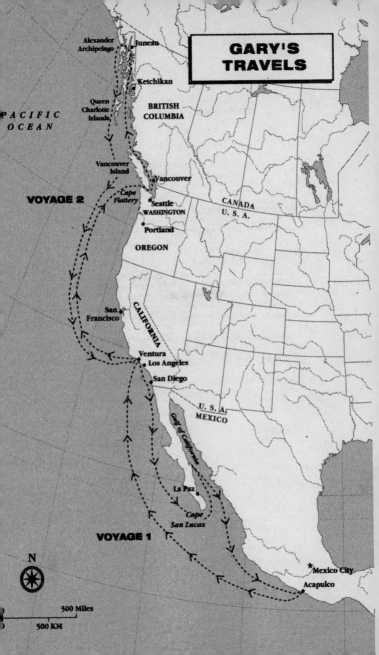

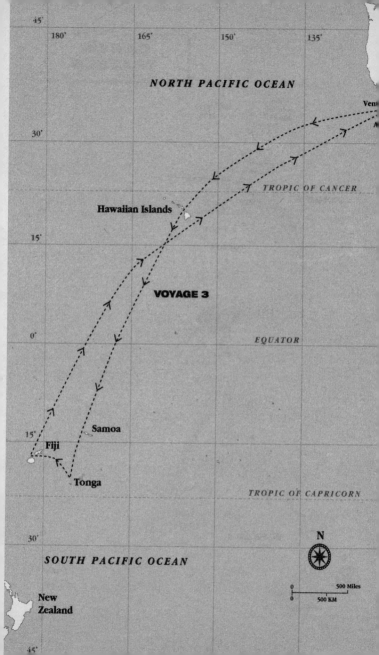

Foreword

The sea was there, deep cobalt, immense, rising like a great saucer to the blue horizon, where it was impossible to see a defining line between water and sky.

It staggered me, stopped my breath, stopped all of me dead on the deck when I first saw it.

I was seven years old on a troopship heading to the Philippine Islands. We had left San Francisco some ten days earlier but I had not seen the ocean yet. I had chicken pox when we left, and my mother and the captain had smuggled me into the ship in the dark, wrapped in a blanket, and kept me in a small cabin without a porthole, down inside the boat so that I could not infect the rest of the crew or the soldiers on board. I stayed there until I was past the infectious stage.

But I had smelled it, the sea, and heard it against the side of the ship at night over the sound of the engine, the *swish-roar* of it down the steel sides and through the propellers at the stern and I knew it was there.

But I had not seen it until just now, when my mother had come down inside the boat to get me, breathlessly telling me that a plane full of people was going to crash near the ship and that I should come to watch.

I did not know how to get out, but I scrambled after her up ladders and through the hatches and down an alleyway until she opened a heavy metal hatch door and we stepped out on the deck, and I stopped dead.

For a second or two the sun off the water and the striking color were so brilliant that they seemed to burn through my eyes into my brain and I didn't truly see anything.

Then my eyes adjusted and it was there before me, blue, grandly blue and huge, filling me with a thrilling joy that completely took me over.

The plane crashed and broke in half near the ship, and the sharks that had been following the troopship moved to the women and children in the water, many of whom were bleeding into the water from injuries. The attack was fast, ripping, savage. Some of the people were killed and many others left with terrible wounds that I would see later when they came aboard the ship from the lifeboats. I was horrified and have written of the horror in another book, but it affected me in a way that I did not fully comprehend then, and did not know until later.

Terrible as it was, I found the attack not frightening but somehow natural, a part of what I was seeing for the first time.

I had heard the sailors talking about sharks. I knew that they attacked things, killed and ate, and were an eternal part of the sea. I marveled at their sleek beauty as they left the ship and moved into the crash area; gray and streamlined, they fit the blue of the water and the bright sun.

Screams and the sounds of people dying filled the air. But even so, I found myself looking out across the expanse of water on the other side of the ship, away from the sinking plane and struggling people.

The water moved up to the sky, beckoning. It pulled me in a way that I knew was important,

even at the age of seven, a way that was pro-
foundly vital and would never leave me.

We were on the slow ship for several weeks as
we took the survivors back to Hawaii and then
sailed on to Okinawa and the Philippines. I spent
uncounted hours sitting at the bow looking at the
water and the sky, studying each wave, different
from the last, seeing how it caught the light, the
air, the wind; watching the patterns, the sweep of
it all, and letting it take me.

The sea.

The First Sail

I was discharged from the army after nearly four years, most of it spent at Fort Bliss, Texas, in May of 1962. I hated every second of my time in the army and although I was still very young, I did not think I could salvage the time I had just wasted, or that I could save my ruined life. I know how ridiculous that sounds now, but the feeling was real then. I remember sitting in my old truck in El Paso, Texas, thinking that I was done, had no future, and the thought popped in out of nowhere that if I didn't see water soon I would die.

Now I'm amazed to remember how much I missed the sea, because it hadn't been a real part of my life between the ages of ten and seventeen, when I enlisted. Maybe I longed for it now because of all the time spent eating sand in the winds of the desert.

I drove to California that very day, straight to the coast, then north, away from people, to a small town named Guadalupe, near Santa Maria. There I bought some cans of beans and bread and Spam and fruit cocktail and a cheap sleeping bag and then walked out through the sand dunes, where I could hear the surf crashing. I walked until I could see the water coming in, rolling in from the vastness, and I sat down and let the sea heal me.

I was there six days and nights. Before dark each night I gathered driftwood for a fire. The salt in the wood makes it slow to burn and it was difficult to light. But I worked at it until there was a good blaze going. I would heat a can of beans and sit there not thinking, really not thinking of anything at all, listening to the waves roll in and licking the salt from the spray off my lips until the heat from the fire made me sleepy. Then I would crawl into my bag near a huge log that must have ridden the Pacific currents down from the British Columbian forests, and I would sleep as if drugged, as if dead.

Today you would see people there. Today

there are developments and beach houses and condos and malls and noise and garbage and oil. But then I saw nobody, heard nothing but the gulls and the crashing sea and now and then the bark of a seal as it hunted the kelp beds just offshore.

It would be easy to say it was peaceful and just drop it there. And it *was* peaceful. Years later I would come to run sled dogs in the North woods, and to run the Iditarod race in Alaska, and there would be moments of incredible serenity then, quiet and cold and peaceful, but nothing quite like that time after the army when the sea saved me.

I went away from there a new person, and I also began to understand things about myself, that I must see and know the oceans. I must go to the sea, as the writers Herman Melville and Richard Henry Dana, Jr., and Ernest K. Gann and Sterling Hayden had done. Like them, I must seek myself there, as the novelist James Jones did as he was writing *Go to the Widow-Maker*.

To do that, I would need a boat.

When first I thought about boats, the intensity and obsessiveness that people brought to them seemed overbearing, silly. Most boat owners I met seemed ridiculously anal and boring—as indeed some of them are.

Except for trapping in the North woods with a canoe, I knew absolutely nothing about boats. I had crossed the Pacific that one time at the age of seven in a navy ship, and my knowledge of that was limited to old, dented steel, the hum of huge engines, and a bunch of kind sailors who wanted me to introduce them to my mother, who was young and lovely and almost terminally seasick.

When I was about fourteen, I made one wild attempt at sailing. In a book on woodcraft I found a drawing of a "sailing canoe" and built a sixteen-foot canvas canoe from a kit that I sent for. It came complete—wood, glue, canvas, nails and paint—for just thirty-one dollars. The book made it seem simple to turn my canoe into a sailboat by rigging a dried pine pole for a mast with a small boom and using an old bedsheet for a sail.

I set it up with the canoe tied to a dock on a lake in northern Minnesota. I tied it fore and aft (though I would not have used those nautical terms yet) so that it was stable. There was a slight breeze blowing from the left rear; later I learned that this is called the stern-port quarter. Following the instructions, I lashed a paddle on the side to act as a leeboard to keep the canoe from sliding sideways, and used the other paddle across the stern to steer the canoe.

Then I untied the lashings (cast off the dock lines), pulled in the rope tied to the end of the boom (which tightened the main sheet), and to my complete surprise the canoe shot away from the dock and started across the lake so fast it made a little bow wave. I slammed the steering paddle across the stern and pushed sideways a bit. The canoe turned, caught even more speed and seemed to leap for the far shore, which lay three or four miles away.

I had time for one gleeful thought of triumph as we zipped to a point almost exactly in the middle of the lake. Then the canoe flipped upside down with a vicious sideways roll that came out of nowhere so fast that I was caught beneath it—my head in the dark—and wondering what had happened. I swam out from under the canoe—it remained afloat because it was made of wood—and struggled to get it back upright. It teetered for an instant and then flopped over the other way, upside down again.

Back and forth we went, like a wounded gull, the sail flopping first left and then right until, finally, I gave up and pulled the mast out, turned the canoe back upright, bailed it out and paddled it back to shore, swearing that I would never, absolutely never, sail again.

So when I first realized I must be on the sea, near the sea, in the sea, I thought of power boats and not sailboats.

Then I began to read about the sea and found that the Pacific Ocean was so enormous it dominated the entire planet; all the land mass in the world could fit inside the Pacific and there would still be sea around it. If I wanted to know this ocean—and I did, desperately—then I needed a kind of vessel that could cover great distances. The only power vessels with adequate fuel capacity were large ships and there was no way I could ever afford to own a ship.

I would have to use a vessel that used free power, the wind. I would have to use a sailboat.

At the time, 1965, I was working in Hollywood, learning to write, and the second thing happened that would change my life forever.

I was part of a low-level party circuit of writers who worked on the fringe of films and were not yet successful. We were always trying to meet the Right People, to be at the Right Place at the Right

Time. (Yes, I believed then that was the way it was done, until I found that it was the opposite of the truth and taught nothing.) A very rich and famous star invited a dozen or so of us up to Lake Arrowhead to his waterfront home for a weekend party. I don't know why he invited us—God knows he didn't know any of us and never spoke to us—but it was exactly the kind of party we thought it was important to attend and we all drove up on Friday night for "a glorious weekend at the lake."

Lake Arrowhead is a semiritzy area, a very small lake in the mountains near Los Angeles, a reservoir lake. Coming from northern Minnesota, where I lived among some fourteen thousand lakes, visiting this one was not particularly exciting for me.

Early Saturday morning, having concluded that the whole thing was a bust, I went for a walk along the shore, killing time until my host woke up and I could tell him I had some urgent reason to go back to the city. I rounded a bend in the shoreline and came upon a wooden dock that stuck out fifty feet into the lake. Tied to the dock was a small sailboat. It had one sail, a main, and no foresail and was about twelve feet long. The sail was up and flopping gently in the soft morning breeze.

Now, except for the slapstick attempt with the canoe, I had no concept of sailing.

There was an older man standing on the dock by the boat and he saw me looking at it and smiled.

"You like to sail?"

I shrugged and shook my head. "I might. I don't know. I've never really done it. . . ."

"You want to try it?"

I nodded. "I sure would."

"Hop in and we'll go out."

I never found out his name, and in view of the effect he had on my life it is a shame, because I owe him a great deal.

The boat (a little cat scow plywood racer) seemed to be a welter of lines running through pulleys and eyes. He motioned me to sit in the front of the small cockpit. "Crouch down so your head won't get hit by the boom when we come about."

"Boom?" I asked. "Come about?"

He pointed to the flopping wooden pole on the bottom edge of the sail. I looked up at it just in time to get hit solidly in the forehead three or four times.

"That's the boom," he said. "It's aptly named."

He motioned for me to let loose the bowline tied to the cleat, and then he pushed the boat away from the dock and pulled a flat, blade-shaped board down in the middle.

The boat wallowed with the two of us squatting there, the sail flopping back and forth, and I didn't see how it could be translated into any kind of movement.

Then he pulled in on the main sheet and the sail filled and he slammed the rudder to the side and the boat suddenly became alive.

I have had similar thrills: I took flying lessons in an Aeronca Champ and when I soloed and the plane left the ground and did that greasy little slide that planes do when they first catch the air, it felt something like this boat did; or when I first ran a large team of sled dogs and they took me out of myself.

But this, this beginning motion, this first time when a sail truly filled and the boat took life and knifed across the lake under perfect control, this was so beautiful it stopped my breath, as it had stopped when I first saw the Pacific.

The man was a master sailor and controlled the

sail with the main sheet, letting it in and out to
compensate for the fluky lake winds, keeping the
boat at a ten- or fifteen-degree heel as it cut across
the lake. Then he jibed effortlessly, brought the
stern across the wind and out the other side, ran
half a mile down the length of the lake before he
tacked in three quick cuts back up, then reached
across and back to the dock, then back and forth
across the lake in easy reaches, moving from one
puff of wind to the next, working the sheet and
the tiller in perfect unison to move from one wind
ruffle on the lake to another, all while I marveled
at his skill.

We never really spoke. I wanted to know a million things but felt so ignorant I was afraid to ask
for fear of sounding too dumb. I didn't even know
enough to ask. But I would think often of him
when I was sailing my own boat and how he
seemed as easy as a gull, working the sail this way
a bit and that way a tiny amount to move with the
wind and catch every little bit of energy there was,
like a bird flying on a light sea breeze without
moving its wings.

Maybe an hour or an hour and a half we sailed.
He came back and dropped me at the dock and
moved off to another part of the lake and I never

saw him again. I walked back to the house and made my excuses and drove back to Hollywood almost in a dream.

I would have to find a boat. Nothing else would matter until I did.

First Boat   2

I bought some magazines and looked in news-
papers at boat ads and found that my ignorance
was worse than I'd thought. There were sailboats
for sale ranging from three hundred dollars to four
or five million dollars.

I was living on less than four thousand dollars
a year, so that pretty much wiped out the four-
million-dollar boats.

I would not just need a sailboat, I would need
a cheap sailboat. This was my first mistake. There
is an old Chinese proverb that states something
like "Cheap isn't really cheap, expensive isn't really
expensive." The concept is that when you think
you're getting something at a very low price,

usually you have to spend so much to fix it that it would have been better to buy the more expensive one in the first place.

Then too, looking for a bargain boat is like playing Russian roulette. If the boat is cheaply made, and run-down enough, it can actually kill you. This is a fairly common occurrence, much more than people generally realize. A single fitting can let go and a boat will sink; a bolt can shear and carry away rigging and take someone down with it. I know of a man who died when a pin let go in a snatch block (a kind of quick-use movable pulley) and the block blew off the line it was holding and came back with such velocity it drove through his forehead, killing him instantly.

Thankfully—or insanely—I did not know any of this. In my innocence and ignorance I put the papers and magazines down and drove up the coast north of Los Angeles and went to a harbor. There I found a yacht brokerage, stopped my old VW bug, walked into a small office where a man sat nursing what must have been a seismic hangover and said, blithely, "I want to buy a sailboat."

The mistakes I was making were appalling. First, trying to save money and going to a "yacht" brokerage were two things that could never work together. Anytime the word *yacht* is used, the boat will cost too much.

Second, walking in and actually saying to a yacht broker that you want to buy a sailboat is like pouring your own blood into water infested with white sharks. You might as well just hand him a knife and tell him to start hacking away at your wallet.

Third, and perhaps most important, never, ever interrupt a man working through a really bad hangover.

He stood, slowly, and shook my hand while looking at me with a distinctly predatory glint in his eye, then proceeded to show me an old, wooden, thirty-two-foot Tahiti ketch that in all kindness should have been cut up and burned for the hardware.

"She's salty," he said, taking me down inside the dank interior. It was a bit like going into a sewer except the smell was worse: something between old sweatsocks, rotten meat and dead fish (I think all three were floating in the bilge).

"A proven sailor," he said. "You could take her to the South Pacific tomorrow, and the beauty of a wood boat over fiberglass is that if you hit a reef and take a plank out, you can repair her right there in the lagoon with whatever wood you can find."

He lied, cleanly, effortlessly, and I did not know that if you take a plank out of a wood boat it sinks. Fast. And that truly old wood boats, as this one was (much older than me), had a nasty habit of "opening up" while under way, popping planks off when fasteners let go, so that water would roar in and they would drive themselves beneath the waves. And sink.

But as he spun tales of the South Pacific, I saw dusky dancing maidens and balmy nights, sliding along with the trade winds caressing our naked bodies while we replaced planks with available wood and let the magic of the tropics take our cares away. . . .

Only a bit of serendipity kept me from buying the boat and sailing off to my doom. We were down inside the boat, which looked nicely nautical with varnished wood and white paint, and I was ready to sign the deal when I noticed a floor panel that seemed to be slightly open. I am ashamed to admit that I had not looked beneath the panels or inside the cupboards, and I leaned forward and pulled the panel up, my head still full of dreams of tropical nights. I was surprised to see water there, welling up. Not just standing in the bilge but grow- ing while I watched, and then an electric pump kicked in and the water level went back down until the pump stopped, when it immediately rose again, pushing at the floor panels, and the pump started again. . . .

The boat would sink in a couple of hours if the automatic bilge pump weren't working. Finally my brain woke up. I decided to look in the bilge and found that the frames holding the planking were so rotten the wood came away in my hand.

"It needs a lick of paint here and there," the broker said. "And maybe tighten a few screws . . ."

I left him there and went to the next brokerage, and the next, finding boats either falling apart or way too expensive for my pocketbook, and quite often both.

I don't know how long this might have gone on. I was there several days, sleeping in my car. I looked at scores of boats and couldn't find anything that would work until I was in the Ventura harbor walking down the docks just looking at boats in general when I came upon a little twenty-two-footer with a tiny wooden bowsprit and a small cabin that had a faded sign hanging on the bow pulpit: For Sale by Owner.

It was a Schock 22, three years old. It was sloop rigged with a keel/centerboard that could be dropped when fighting against the wind, what's called beating to windward.

She had a tiny cabin less than five feet high, a small wooden table and two bunks, a little alcohol stove, a head (toilet) up in the middle of the forepeak; and (best of all) she was made of fiberglass. This was before soft cores and more flexible hulls, and she was handcrafted of fiberglass nearly an inch thick. In most respects she was nearly bulletproof. Later, through ineptness, I ran her into a dock at four knots while trying to sail into the slip and all she did was dent the wood of the dock and bounce off.

I called the owner and he agreed to let me pay her off over time. I moved on board and slept in the boat that first night and dreamed of the South Pacific and the trade winds, and I awakened the next morning and made coffee and sat there in the cockpit thinking that all I had to do now was learn to sail and I was ready to go.

Just that, learn to sail.

No problem.

People did it all the time. How hard could it be?

* * *

Of course, there are many degrees of sailing ability. It is an art, most assuredly, and it is an art that you can develop for the rest of your life; you will never learn it all because wind and sails and water are different at all times.

Still, everybody must start somewhere. Had I known how truly ignorant I was, I think I would have given it all up as a bad job.

I had never sailed on the ocean.

I did not know anything about boats.

I did not know anything about the sea.

I did not know any of the terminology and couldn't tell a block from a pintle. The first time somebody said something about the sheets, I thought they were talking about the sails.

But I had a boat, and thanks to pure luck and the honesty of the man who sold her to me, she was a very good boat, with seven different sails and a solid anchoring system, and all in all was in very fine shape, maintenance up to date, everything stowed clean.

So I sat on her that sunny morning in Ventura, California, and I felt a soft breeze on my cheek while I sipped coffee and I thought, I have to take her out sailing. Or, to be more accurate, I thought, I have to take *it* out sailing, because I had not yet come to understand how boats are alive and are always "she."

I looked up at the mast. It was wooden and seemed exceptionally tall. (It turned out that she *was* slightly overpowered, which was very nice in light airs because she got a lot of power out of very little wind. But it was bad in heavy winds because she was so tender, that is, so sensitive to the wind.) There were lines and ropes and cables going all over the place: some kind of rope going up the mast and down to the front sail and then another kind of rope going up the mast and down to the mainsail and then two ropes coming from the front sail bag back to little round winch things in the cockpit and then a whole cluster of ropes and pulleys that seemed to control the back of the boom thing.

All right, I remember thinking, let's start with what I know.

I knew the boom thing held the bottom of the big sail. Then I understood that the pulleys at the back of the boom controlled where it would go. Then I followed the rope that pulled the mainsail up and found where it would tie off on the mast. Okay, I could pull up the main.

I threw back the rest of my coffee, put the cup

on the table down inside the boat next to my type-writer and started the proceedings that would lead to what I later termed the First Disaster.

The boat had a small outboard on the back, or stern, and I checked the fuel, found it full, gave the cord a yank. It fired straight off.

A good start.

Then I threw off the dock lines and pushed the boat back into the space between the two rows of docks and clambered back into the cockpit. I in-creased the throttle and she started to move for-ward. She had a tiller as opposed to a wheel, and I slapped the handle over and brought her nose out into the opening of the fairway that led to the breakwaters at the harbor mouth. I had little sense but enough to know not to put the sails up in the dock, and when we were in the open I stopped the motor, went to the rope, or halyard, that pulled up the main and yanked it up with all my strength.

How I got this far without a real problem is hard to understand, but it was about here that my ignorance really kicked in.

The main was much larger than the sail I had seen at Lake Arrowhead, and as soon as it was up it filled with the morning breeze and slammed over to the side. I had not loosened the sheet, and so the boat, light and quick, took off immediately, playing off to the left as the tiller swung over. I was working up at the right side of the mast and was dumped cleanly off the boat, falling through the two little lifelines into the muck of the harbor, where I treaded water and watched my new sailboat go off without me.

After sailing thirty or forty yards she plowed into the rocks of the shoreline, narrowly missing the right hull of a trimaran that was tied to the end of a dock just adjacent to the opening. I swam to my boat and climbed in and got her moving again, until I hit the trimaran—the Second Disaster. That was just three hours before I hit the million-dollar yacht—the Third Disaster—and was chewed out by a woman who had a martini in one hand and a cigarette hanging out the side of her mouth around which flowed a stream of obscenities I had not heard since my military days. Sometime later I barely caught the edge of a Coast Guard cutter, whose skipper was quite nice and only gave me a courtesy ticket for not having a bell on my boat, although I'm not sure that at this stage of my sailing development a bell would have done me a great deal of good. Not nearly as much good as a few dozen rubber bumpers to hang around the boat.

On the negative side, by the end of the first day I had still not left the harbor and was tied up to the courtesy dock because the motor would not start, and I did not have a clue as to how I could sail the boat back against the wind and into my slip at the dock. On the positive side, I had learned to put the mainsail up and get it down in a hurry—a big hurry. I had met lots of people, some of whom wanted to kill me and several of whom tried to help me, and I had learned to sail the boat in something approximating a straight line and to make it turn—come about—without wetting myself or screaming, although none of this happened with any apparent plan or thought or regularity. Indeed, the boat seemed to have a mind of its own, and several times I found myself wrapped up and entangled in ropes in a helpless mess and looked up to see us (I already thought of the boat and me as something of a team, albeit a poorly trained one) heading into a dock full of boats and screaming people.

I had still not brought up the second sail, the jib, and the thought of doing it froze me cold. I would have terrified half the harbor if they'd known I was going to try it.

It was coming on to late evening, and I

suddenly remembered the prime beauty of living on a boat—that I had everything with me necessary to life and didn't have to go back to my dock. I decided to call it a day and spend the night at the courtesy dock.

When it became evident that I was going to stop for the day, the harbor settled down—people had stationed themselves at the ends of docks and slips with boat hooks to fend me off—and as they went back to their normal lives I found myself caught up in the mystical qualities of living on a boat on the sea.

I had made a trip on a boat and was spending the night at a different place.

True, the trip had been a series of calamities punctuated by terror, and I had only come a total of about three hundred yards from my home dock.

But still, I *had* traveled, and I *was* in a different place and had gotten there by sailing, and I was closer to the harbor mouth, to the sea, the reason for it all. I could see the jetties and the open sea from the courtesy dock, just a hundred and fifty yards away, and as I went below and crouched and crawled around, heating a can of beans on the alcohol stove, I felt the return of the excitement that had come over me as a child on the troopship, the excitement that has never really left me.

The sea was right there, right *there;* I could see it out the small porthole over the stove, and as I crawled into my sleeping bag on the side bunk I thought that tomorrow was another day and I would go out there tomorrow, out of the harbor in the morning, and renew my old acquaintance.

As it happened it came sooner.

The Open Sea   3

I never sleep so soundly as I do on a boat after a hard day of work. The motion of the boat is like a cradle, and as the bunk rocks gently, the brain shuts down.

This was how my first true night on the boat began, but sometime later, when the tide changed and began to flood, I was awakened. The motion had changed as the current started into the harbor, and the boat took a slight roll with the surge that came in. I pulled myself out of the bunk and stuck my head up out of the companionway.

"Oh . . ." The sound escaped me, almost a sigh. The sky was clear and the moon—how had I not seen it earlier?—had come out full and bright. It

was so beautiful it didn't seem real, almost con-
trived in some fashion, as if nature were showing
off by making the perfect sea-night. There were
stars splattered all over the sky, dim near the
moon, sparkling brightly away from the splash of
white light, and across the sea and through the jetties and straight into the boat slashed a silver bar
of reflected light from the moon.

I had to be out there.

I could not let that beauty simply go to waste. I
pulled on my clothes, and a jacket since it was
fairly cool. For the first time in my life I truly paid
attention to the wind.

There was a slight offshore breeze of four, five
knots, no more, blowing out from the dock to the
harbor mouth. Perfect.

Earlier in the day the motor had quit on me.
Before going to bed I'd discovered that a small
rubber fuel line had vibrated loose, and I'd repaired it. I pulled the starter rope three times before it started, then untied the dock lines and idled
away from the dock toward the harbor mouth,
moving straight up the bar of moonlight.

We were moving with the wind, about the
same speed as the wind, so there would be no
force on the sail. I tied a line around the tiller han-

dle to hold it in position and pulled the mainsail up and cleated the halyard off and was even more amazed by the beauty of the moonlight as it reflected off the white sail.

I could have read in this light. I was almost dazzled by it, and by the sea. I leaned back on the tiller to take it all in when a gentle swell worked through the harbor mouth.

It was as if the boat took its first breath with the swell. The nose moved up, slid gently down, and she came to life.

Horatio Nelson, the famous English naval hero, once was supposed to have said: "Men and ships rot in port."

Of course, he may have meant it literally, ports being what they are and men and old wooden ships being what *they* are, but I suspect he meant much more by it. Except for some rare bad designs, boats are not meant to live their lives tied to a dock in still water. It is a sad fact that most of them seem to spend their lives in just that way. On the California coast alone there are tens of thousands of sailboats and yet it is common to be out on a very nice weekend, sailing along fifty or sixty miles of coastline, and see only half a dozen boats outside the harbor.

Boats are designed to sail in open water and they do not come alive until then. I had never known this until that first night as I slid past the jetties in the moonlight and felt her take the sea.

It is an astonishing feeling, one that quickens me, makes my breath come softly.

The motor suddenly became an intrusion, an ugly sound, and as soon as I was past the jetties and was in open ocean I killed it. For a few seconds, half a minute, we moved on in silence by inertia, coasting from the energy the motor had given us, and then it died and I felt the breeze again on my face as I looked to the rear. It was pushing at the back edge of the sail and I pulled the tiller over to steer off the wind a bit and felt the sail fill. The boat moved differently now, started the dance with the wind and water and moonlight as she heeled slightly and took on life, personality. We glided along in near silence, the only sound the soft gurgle of water along the hull.

I did not dare to walk forward in the dark and put up the jib, having never done it before, but she sailed pretty well on the mainsail alone and we kept our course, moving at three or four knots by the speedometer in the cockpit, until daylight some four hours away, when the wind stopped, entirely, and left the dawning ocean as still as a pond and me marooned some twelve miles offshore.

I didn't care. I was completely enraptured by what had happened to me. I lowered the mainsail and sat peacefully drifting around in circles, feeling at home, truly at home.

For the entire morning there was no wind, and while I might have had enough gas to motor partway back to the harbor, there was something wrong about using it on such a beautiful morning. I made a small pot of oatmeal on the little stove and some instant coffee and ate breakfast in the cockpit, letting the morning sun warm me; then I pulled my sleeping bag out of the cabin and laid it in the cockpit and took a small sleep while the boat rocked gently on the swells.

A sound awakened me an hour or so later and I looked over the side to see the boat surrounded by swarms of small fish, maybe anchovies or herring. No sooner did I spot them than pelicans came in and began crash-diving around the boat and then other seabirds arrived, and within minutes a huge pod of dolphins, hundreds of them, showed up. The dolphins began working the school of bait fish, sweeping back and forth like happy wolves, thrashing the water with their tails, perhaps to stun the fish. Then they ate them by the thousands.

While I lay in the calm, all around the boat the sea seethed with life. After the dolphins came some sharks, three or four on call to clean up the debris from the slaughter. In half an hour they were gone, moving off, following the schools of small fish and dolphins and flocks of seabirds.

"Amazing," I said aloud. It was amazing that I would be greeted on the sea with such enthusiasm, amazing that on one of the most populated coasts in the world, near a metropolis that stretched nearly two hundred miles from San Diego to Santa Barbara, where nearly eighteen million people jammed the freeways and sidewalks, I would be completely alone with the sea and my boat; amazing that the planet still held such a place.

Learning to Sail   4

It was a strange way to start sailing. I had flailed and collided my way around the harbor, finally got the boat to move after a fashion, then sailed into the open sea in the dark. And now there was no wind.

All day.

But there were things happening, and if I'd had any knowledge of the sea, they would have meant something to me. The ocean had started almost unbelievably flat, no waves, almost no swell. After dozing for a time and awakening and making more coffee, I noticed the boat starting to rock more than it had during the night and early morning.

This meant nothing to me. It should have meant the world for it could be a matter of life and death. But at the time I thought, A little more swell out of the west, so what? There was no wind, no waves. I had the seabirds for company. . . .

Except that I didn't. The seabirds were gone now and had I been noticing I would have seen that they had all flown inland, flocks of them flying into sheltered waters, settling on protected back-waters and in harbors.

Had I been more aware I would have known that on this coast at this time of the year—early fall—the prevailing wind was out of the northwest but that now and then there was a very strong off-shore wind, called Santa Ana, and that it was sometimes followed by strong clearing westerlies. The offshore winds could easily hit fifty to seventy knots, and the clearing westerlies could veer, with a strong northerly component, and could run forty to fifty knots when they came up.

The coast here ran almost straight east and west and I was twelve miles offshore, near the south end of a small island named Anacapa, where there was no good anchorage, though it wouldn't have mattered since I'd never anchored and hadn't any idea if the boat even had an anchor. (It did, a good Danforth with two hundred feet of new nylon line and thirty feet of chain.) I was about to get hit by a full gale.

People get in trouble this way and often die through ignorance and foolishness. Over the years that I've been sailing, I have seen dozens of people killed because they did the wrong thing at the wrong time. But ignorance is also bliss, and in the truest sense of the word I was ignorant of my impending doom and living in what could only be termed a kind of bliss.

God, how I had missed the sea! The smell of it, the feel and sound of it took me now, and as the unheeded swells grew larger I rolled around half the day and explored the boat—an act that saved my life.

Though the boat rocked a great deal in the wind and waves, I finally figured out how to put the foresail up. It was hanked on, and for some reason I had difficulty figuring out how it worked, so I put it on and took it off several times as we rolled wildly, with no wind to steady the boat in the swells, hanging on to the stay with one hand while I worked with the other. (I know it is a sailor's cliché, but it was my first time to run into the concept: one hand for yourself, one for the ship.)

The centerboard was heavy, made of steel, and kept banging around in the partial keel that hung down, so I used the ratchet crank inside the boat, mounted to the end of the small table, and cranked the board up tightly into its housing. Another act that may have helped to save my life.

By now it was past noon and the swells were almost vicious. Without force of wind the boat would not steer or lie to, and she wound up lying almost perfectly sideways to the swells, which were six and eight feet high, with about seven seconds between them.

I looked to shore, more than twelve miles off, and thought maybe I should use the motor to head back. This came under the heading of far too little action far too late to do any good. The motor was a small five-horse that moved the boat at perhaps four knots in a harbor, an in-and-out-of-the-slip motor. It would do nothing against waves. And besides, there was enough gas to take the boat only six or seven miles in a dead calm. In waves we might even move backward.

And now, at last, came the wind.

A touch on my cheek, a small zephyr, enough to slat the sails, fill them, let them pull a bit and then flop again. I had both the main and the jib up by now and I remember being confident, almost cocky, and I thought that if it would only start to blow harder maybe I could learn how it worked when a sailboat sailed against the wind. This was utter folly—teasing fate by actually *hoping* for a hard wind.

The wind freshened still more and the sails flapped louder until I pushed the tiller over and they filled and the boat slid forward, suddenly alive, one, two, then three knots on the speedometer in the cockpit.

It's happening, I thought. It's all working—I'm sailing. I pulled on the main sheet, pointed the boat higher into the wind and actually found myself tacking back toward shore, against the wind. I let the jib sheet out and the speed decreased; I pulled it back in and it increased.

Astonishing, I thought. Could it all really be this easy, this simple?

I looked past the bow at the sea and saw small waves forming as the boat sailed forward into them, slamming into them, spray coming back into my face. Incredible, wonderful, amazing.

And then the first inkling: out there, far ahead of the bow, almost on the horizon, it seemed as if a knife were cutting off the tops of the waves.

Clean, flat, almost surgical, shearing the tops away neatly, and I thought, there it is, the wind, the big wind—just as it seemed to skip the intervening miles between us and slammed into the boat.

I had been in overpowering situations before—I'd nearly frozen to death while hunting and had also watched a typhoon hit the Philippines—but I had never felt so completely at the mercy of natural forces.

The boat slammed, tore, *ripped* sideways across the water. She was knocked flat. Without instrumentation I had no way of knowing the speed but I suspect that the beginning of the blow was more than sixty knots.

It was extraordinary that the sails didn't blow out and shred. At the time the idea of Dacron sails was new (many boats still used cotton), and my Dacron sails were oversewn and overbuilt and incredibly strong.

Actually, the fact that they didn't shred added to my peril. The sails filled from the beam and drove the boat over on her side and then kept her there. I went from sitting idly in the cockpit, daydreaming about stronger wind, to hanging on to a winch, looking across the cockpit straight *down* into the water.

The waves immediately increased and became four feet of crosswave on top of the rolling swells, which were already eight or ten feet. The boat lay on her side, held down by the sails, covered by waves that threatened to sweep me out of the cockpit, and I hadn't a clue as to what to do to save myself; at any second I expected her to capsize and roll and fill and sink. I knew I would drown, for it was impossible to swim in such waves even with a life jacket on, and I didn't have a life jacket. I thought, How could this be? How could you die just a few miles out on a sunny day while people are sitting right over there in their homes watching the pretty sailboat sink?

The boat slid down a large wave, hesitated in the trough, seemed to shudder, then, still on her side (in a condition known as blowdown) floated to the top of the next wave, which covered me with water. She stayed there only a moment, then slid sickeningly down sideways into the next trough, shuddered, then repeated the cycle.

What was saving the boat, and almost incidentally me, was the fact that in my ignorance I had cranked the centerboard up into its housing. Had it still been down in the fully extended position, it would probably have caught and "tripped" the boat and almost certainly resulted in a capsizing. The boat would have filled and I would have drowned.

As it was, she was in a state of "lying a-hull," just leaving a boat to find her own way through a problem—a survival procedure I used in ignorance and would come to detest and never use again with any boat. I was in great peril because the sails were still up. The normal procedure for lying a-hull is to douse all sails and tie them down with gaskets, batten all hatches and go below.

I was well past any decent part of my learning curve and simply hung in the cockpit, looking down in horror and a kind of numbness at the slate blue water roiling by beneath me. I thought suddenly of when I had crossed the Pacific, this same ocean, on that troopship when I was seven years old and how peaceful it had been, how blue and soft and inviting, the waves small and gentle.

I saw blood in the cockpit, smearing down the wet fiberglass, and wiped my face to find I had slammed into something and had a cut on my forehead and a first-class nosebleed. I hadn't felt a thing and couldn't feel it now.

A larger wave hit me like a bus. There are some waves that dwarf others when their move-

ment becomes synchronized and they come together to form a much larger one. In large seas
such swells are known as rogue waves and can be
truly devastating, reaching heights of thirty or even
sixty feet. In World War II such a wave hit an air-
craft carrier in the Atlantic and peeled the flight
deck back like the top of a sardine can.

This wave was perhaps two times the height of
the usual waves hitting me, about eighteen or
twenty feet.

I had time for one word—it may have been a
prayer; I hope it was—and I was under water.

Somehow the wave did not pour down into the
companionway and fill the boat. That would have
sunk us.

But I saw the deep green light through the
water pouring over me and it jarred me out of my
panic-induced stupor.

Another such wave could easily be the end of
us. I had to do something, fix something, save the
boat, save myself.

But what? What did the professionals do when
this happened?

All right, I thought. What is the trouble? What is
causing my difficulties?

The waves.

The waves were too big.

Fine, I thought. I know a thing, I know this. The waves are too big.

Of course there was nothing I could do to make them smaller.

What else?

The wind—it was too strong. It was blowing the boat over, so I was being driven even further by the waves that were too big. And as with the waves, I could do nothing to reduce the wind.

What else?

I couldn't change the wind but perhaps I could reduce the effect of the wind on the boat.

I could—a revelation—reduce the area of the sail. I could pull down the sails. I could reef.

When I looked at the mainsail, lying almost horizontal to the sea, there seemed no way to make it come down. Then I saw the gearing where the boom joined the mast, truly noticed it for the first time; the boat had what was called worm-gear roller reefing, which meant I had to somehow stand up by the mast and lower the sail rope (halyard) with one hand, while slowly working a crank that rotated the boom with the other hand, while clinging to the boat with my teeth and rolling the mainsail up on the boom the way a window shade is raised. It is a system designed by a maniac advised by a madman who apparently never considered reefing a boat anywhere but tied up at the dock, and I wished fervently he was there at that moment.

I looked at the front of the boat. It was almost constantly under water, thick spray followed by the tops of waves, green water.

I must go up there, I thought, and hang on and crank and let the sails down.

It isn't going to happen.

The thoughts came together. I must do it. It can't be done. I must do it. It can't be done.

It was my first real exposure to the fundamental truth of nature, the overriding law that governs all: man proposes; nature, in all her strength and glory, disposes.

The wind and waves did not care about me, did not care about the boat; we could live, we could die. It didn't matter to nature, no more than when nature finds other ways—disease, avalanche, fire or just falling rocks—to kill you.

I was playing in nature's playground perhaps for the first true time in my life, and there were no rules. I could get lucky, I could get unlucky.

So, scared as I was, exposed as I was, alone as

I was, whether I did it out of bravery or fear, whether I got lucky or didn't, I had no choice. If I didn't go up there and lower the sails I would surely get creamed by the next extreme wave, or the one after that.

I had to go.

And yet . . .

And yet . . .

What with exploding missiles in the army, the Iditarod dog race in Alaska, some rough horses and close calls on motorcycles, I've been exposed to plenty of danger. Sometimes I've done it voluntarily and sometimes I've been forced into it, but to this day I have never been as reluctant to do a thing as I was to go out and lower the sails on the small foredeck of that little boat lying sideways on the water.

I would later hear men die on the sea, would hear them on the radio when no help could get to them and they knew it was the end, would hear in every word they said, the resignation in their voices, the last and basic and true understanding of what was coming, and I felt that way this time. It just did not look possible.

And yet . . .

There were ropes hanging about everywhere:

loose sheets, ends of dock lines I had not stowed properly, scraps knocked out of seat lockers by the wild motion. I found one about thirty feet long and I made a loop under my armpits and then tied the other end to a sheet cleat in the cockpit. It left me enough slack to get up to the mast and, I hoped, would give me something to grab and pull myself back with if I went over the side. All of this was wrong. I know now that I should have had a jack-line—safety line—rigged and should have had a good safety harness and should not have gone to sea without them. If I went over the side with a thirty-foot rope around my waist, my chances of pulling myself back to the boat in that wind and sea were virtually zero. Climbing back in could cripple me even before I drowned.

With the decision to try and do something, my brain had started to work again, to a limited degree, and I looked at the sails, both of them almost lying in the water on the port side, and I realized I would not only have to lower them but do something with them after they were lowered.

Tie them up.

The main had been tied to the boom with small webbing gaskets, and I had thrown them down inside on the port bench when I pulled the main up.

I looked down inside the tiny cabin. Everything that hadn't been tied down was upside down and had crashed into the downward side of the boat in a pile, and several dollops of waves had gone in and turned it all into a sodden mass. It was my first exposure to the number one law of the sea: If given a chance a container of oatmeal will open, mix with an open container of coffee grounds, further combine itself with eight or ten gallons of seawater and then find its way into your sleeping bag. The same law states that *all* silverware will fall out of *all* drawers or containers and you will only find half of it, no matter how long you have the boat or how hard you look for it. (This is not to be confused with the second law of the sea, which says that the head will always plug itself at the most disgusting time and do so with the most disgusting object possible.)

I had to find something to use for restraining the sails, so I pulled myself into the cabin opening and reached into the mess and started throwing things around and had not been at it long when I saw the end of one of the yellow gaskets. When I pulled at it the other two came up with it and I untangled them and looped them around my neck (note: I could easily have hanged myself).

Back in the cockpit I looked at the sails. To-gether they were too much, I thought. One at a time. One at a time.

I had the gaskets to tie the mainsail down; we would do that one first.

I looked forward once more, and as I did the boat took a downward lurch and a wave swept across her bow, part of it actually going *over* the top of the mainsail as it lay in the water, dragging it further down.

But she righted herself and as she did I noticed there was a time, a few moments, when she swung up past the horizontal and actually brought the sail slightly up into the air. It did not last long, and she was nowhere near upright, but there was a lessen-ing to her sideways look, and I waited for the next such motion, half a minute, and when it came I scuttled crablike, hanging on with hands and feet and, it seemed, with teeth as well, as the boat slammed up and down in the waves, torn by the wind.

After three attempts I finally clawed the main halyard loose from the cleat that held it and unfas-tened it. Had I expected the main to come down by itself, as it did in calmer weather in the harbor, I would have been sadly disappointed. It did not drop at all and I knew I would have to drag it down. By this time the boat had gone virtually horizontal again and I was lying facedown on top of the mast looking into the water.

I waited for the next roll and when it came I reached over my head and dragged at the main where the slides met the mast track and pulled three or four feet of sail to me, then waited for the next roll, and when we came up again I pulled another hunk of sail and kept this up until I saw the top of it four feet over my head.

I did not have lazy jacks (a kind of rope-cradling system to catch the sail when it comes down) and consequently the sail flopped out to the side in the water and seemed as if it would drag the boat under when it filled. But luckily the wind load was gone, and though the loose sail in the water looked terrible, much of the pressure had been reduced and the boat came up closer to an even keel.

I do not mean to give the impression that there was any semblance of order. The boat was still out of control, pitching wildly, slamming its bow under the waves. The mainsail lay over in the water, lines went everywhere (the tail of the main halyard had gotten away from me and was tangled in the spreaders), the jib was still full and dragging the boat around, which was *not*, as books on sailing would have it, ". . . rounding handily up into the wind." No, the boat pitched and tossed because one of the loose lines or sheets had fouled the tiller handle over to the side, which kept the bow well off the wind and the foresail filled.

I was hanging on to the mast with one hand, the gaskets around my neck, trying to snag the sail and get it out of the water, when the boom decided to kill me.

The main sheet had, of course, long been lost to me, so it was not controlling the boom. With the sail collapsed in the water there was no tension at all on the boom and it started to sweep back and forth, clearing the deck. I was at the mast, out of the way, but to catch the sail I would have to move out away from the mast where the boom could get me, and as soon as I moved it caught me in the middle of the chest and swept me off the boat. I hung on and when it came back I got my feet back on the boat and dragged at the mainsail again, timing my effort to avoid the sweeping boom until at last I had a big enough chunk of the main to tie up with a gasket. It was probably only four or five minutes of intense, painful, impossibly wet effort, but it seemed like a lifetime. This pulled much of the rest of the main out of the water and the next large area came up a bit easier; I tied it off and then I attacked the jib.

It was a thing possessed. It would fill with a slamming explosion, then slap empty, then refill, and I undid the halyard without really knowing what to expect. I was amazed to see it drop a bit between fill-slams. The piece of rope I had put around my waist was not long enough to allow me to get up to the jib so I found another loose sheet, tied it around my waist and to the mast, untied the first piece of rope, and on my hands and knees crawled out on the tiny foredeck to find that the jib came down surprisingly easily. I wadded it into a bundle and used my remaining gasket to tie it all to the side of the little bow pulpit.

I crawled back to the mast, untied the second sheet from my waist, retied the first line from the cockpit and crawled back to the cockpit.

Everything was still on the edge of disaster. Yet the boat, while slamming mightily, had found a way to heave to with the wind pushing her bow while the still-fouled tiller held her off (a good foul-weather maneuver, though I hadn't known what it was called or how it was done). I could tell

that the boat had settled into a mode that somehow took care of her and kept her at least partially
sensible, so I decided the best thing I could do
was go below and try to straighten her up a bit
and get some rest.

It was coming on to dark, and the wind and
waves, if anything, had increased. I went below
into the dank hold of the cabin to find everything
wet and the water up to the floorboards. There
was a little hand bilge-pump affair with a hose that
extended into the cockpit and I pumped for half
an hour until the intake sucked dry.

My sleeping bag was soaked but I crawled into
the forward V-bunk and pulled it over me and
used a seat cushion for a pillow, and even with the
wet bag, my cuts and bruises and a huge quantity
of fear, as soon as my eyes closed I was asleep. I
was so tired it was difficult to breathe, and I had
every intention of sleeping until it was over.

It was not to be.

After maybe two hours the boat was hit by
what seemed like a freight train. The blow
slammed me over to the side against the hull and
woke me up in pitch darkness to sense/see a huge
quantity of water coming in the companionway.

I had just sat up and it drove me back down. I

was sure we were sinking. I sputtered and came up and saw that water had once again covered the floor boards. I manned my little bilge pump in the darkness and pumped for hours, until it sucked dry.

Outside it was madness. I had heard wind make a sound in the rigging before—in the marina, where ten or fifteen knots made a keening sound. Now it shrieked deafeningly, and the waves hit the boat again and again, driving her back so hard that the low cockpit filled and the drains couldn't keep up and the water ran out of the low scuppers in a flood.

In my misery and panic I'd forgotten the three boards that closed the companionway. They were lying on the floor and I found them in the dark by feel. And about the dark: There must have been clouds hiding the moon, because there was a complete absence of light. I had once been deep in the Carlsbad Caverns when they killed the light and this darkness, like that, was total. My eyes would not get used to it, and even when I stuck my head up into the ripping madness outside I could not see, only sense, the towering waves.

I had been frightened before, panicked. But now the darkness and the increase in the strength of the storm combined to terrify me. It did not seem possible to survive.

And yet . . .

The boat rose on each wave, rose and hung and lived and slid backward to fill her little cockpit, to hang there, back heavy, while the water drained, to rise again and hang and live. To live.

I came to love the boat. Not over time, not over long days of beautiful sailing, not over a period of learning, but *right then* I came to love her and thought of her as "she" and the two of us as "we" and knew where the thinking came from, knew that it was not silliness but an honest and logical truth: Had she not been alive, had she not risen and held and worked with the sea, I would have been dead. She must be a living thing to act so, and I would never again make fun of anybody who called a boat "she." (Twenty years later, when I ran the Iditarod with a lead dog named Cookie who saved me not once but several times, I came to love her so much that I always thought of us as "we.")

The boat had a light, a bulb in the ceiling fed by a single twelve-volt battery. The battery was really for the running lights but the boat designer had thrown in a ceiling connection as well. Along with many things I had forgotten about the ceiling bulb and the battery, and I now turned on the power switch, hit the bulb switch and to my complete amazement the inside of the boat was flooded with light.

This accomplished two distinctly opposite things: First, it made me feel good because I could see. Second, it made me feel horrible because I could see. The inside of the boat was a total shambles and would require hours to clean up. Worse, the light shining out of the companionway lit up the area behind the boat just as she slid backward down a wave, and I could see the enormous swell ready to descend on us.

I actually closed my eyes, thinking that this, finally, in this long day and night of horror, was it.

And yet . . .

She filled her cockpit again and she drained again and she rose again. I did not see how she could possibly have survived the wave but I opened my eyes and put the boards in and blocked the companionway and looked at my watch. It was three in the morning and there wasn't a single cell in my body that wasn't completely exhausted. I turned off the light and crawled forward into the V-bunk again and closed my eyes. The sudden darkness seemed to bring the sound of the wind to its height again, along with the roar of the waves as they passed, so I turned the light on once more to sit looking at nothing, at everything around me. Finally I dozed and must have fallen over on the bunk, because when I came to, the boat was rolling gently and a shaft of incredibly hot sunlight was shining in my face through one of the small portholes.

I sat up, pulled the boards out of the companionway and climbed up to the cockpit to a new world of bright sun, blue water, seabirds and, as I watched, two dolphins that came leaping toward the boat to see if there was a bow wave they could ride.

Except for the mess in and on the boat, it was as if none of it had happened. I had done it, I thought, I had weathered a storm. Then I remembered, and thought, no, *we* did it; *we* came through the storm.

And I set about cleaning the boat and trying to head back to the harbor.

Lost at Sea 5

This wild initiation into sailing at sea gave me an accelerated education, though I made many mistakes and misread almost every important cue or clue.

Actually, it had not been a storm but a strong offshore wind, and the waves did not really have the distance required (the "fetch") to become truly dangerous. Nor was the wind that bad. Probably the gusts never exceeded fifty or sixty knots and the constant wind, forty. Lord knows it made sail handling hard enough; for those of you who wish to get a feel for it, get in a car and bring it up to fifty miles an hour and then stick your head and arms outside and, while driving, try to fold up a

simple bath towel in the wind. Then imagine a
huge sail and snaking ropes in the same blast, plus
slamming around in the waves, and you get something of an idea of how hard it can be.

But it was never really dangerous. I was never
at risk except from my own idiocy. It's true you
can drown in a cup of water, but you really have
to work at it, and the same thing was true of my
experience. Looking at it one way, I was working
at destroying myself, and the boat worked equally
hard at saving me. Had I done nothing but crawled
down inside the boat and sucked my thumb—
which had occurred to me—I would probably
have survived just fine.

But at the time I thought that I had weathered a
mighty blow and was probably close to being
ready to go around Cape Horn. At the very least I
must be on the edge of being a master sailor. Had
I stopped to think, I would have remembered
what Longfellow said: "Those whom the Gods
would destroy they first make mad."

But it was not a time for thought so much as
it was a time for action. (Yes, I thought you might
be able to do them exclusively). I decided I should
pay attention to where I was and what to do
about it.

I was lost, that's what I was.

All I knew was that I was still on the Pacific Ocean. I thought I had been driven some distance to the southwest by the blow. I did not have a VHF radio, or a portable radio for music since transistors were not that common yet. I did not have a chart or a sextant or tables to use with a sextant—not that I knew how to use a chart or sextant.

I did have a compass, so I could tell direction. Since I had hunted and fished my whole childhood and had done orientation courses in the army, that was not a problem.

Land, I thought, was over there, to the east. To the west was, presumably, Hawaii and, somewhere beyond that, Asia.

So I had to go east.

The problem, one I have found throughout my sailing life, was that the wind was either feast or famine. It blew too hard for some eighteen or twenty hours. Now it didn't blow at all. Not a breath. The waves quickly died to a flat oily roll and the boat wallowed.

I was not going anywhere for now.

This was another indication of my ignorance. Actually, the blow had taken me southwest close to eighty miles, which, coupled with the fifteen or so I had come before the wind hit me, meant I was now ninety to a hundred miles away from the harbor.

And there was a healthy two-knot current taking me further south and slightly west. I would lie becalmed for days, thinking all the time that I was somewhere west and not too far south of Ventura.

By then I would be some two hundred and fifty miles south of Ventura—about forty miles south of Ensenada, Mexico, on the Baja peninsula, and roughly fifty miles off the coast.

Since the prevailing wind, if it ever came up, was from the west/northwest (that is, out of the west but with a goodly northern component), I would be sailing partially against the wind trying to get home, so that eventually the two hundred and fifty miles that I didn't know about would become close to four hundred miles that I would actually have to sail.

But ignorance was still a form of bliss and I spent the next three days drying my sleeping bag and the cushions and taking stock of my supplies, and I use the word *supplies* with a great deal of latitude.

By a fluke of good fortune I had just filled the fresh-water tank on the boat. It held twenty gallons and fed to a small sink by the companionway and was drawn by a little hand pump on the faucet. The water tasted of hose, or fiberglass, but it was good.

Food was a bit more of a problem. If my memory serves I had four fairly large cans of Chef Boyardee spaghetti and meatballs, three cans of sardines, one loaf of salt-water-soaked bread, a small box of sugar cubes and a small jar of instant coffee. I think there was also a can of pork and beans, heavy on the beans. I'd also had one small box of oatmeal, but when the wave hit us the oatmeal opened and mixed with the water to form a paste that I would be cleaning out of the boat's corners (and bilge-pump strainers) for weeks.

That first day after the storm I was famished. Since I would presumably soon be back at the harbor, I ate a full can of spaghetti and, later that day, a can of sardines on a piece of salty bread dried on top of the companionway hatch.

On the second day I ate the can of beans, but on the third day of lying there, with the sun cooking and drying everything out, a cautionary switch went off in my brain and I ate nothing but drank probably a gallon of water. Hunger set in heavily; I was a hearty eater and used to regular meals because I'd just gotten out of the army and hadn't started to starve as a writer yet.

On the fourth day there was some wind. It was flukey and light but I untied the main and pulled it and the jib up and put ninety degrees on the compass and headed, I thought, for Ventura—just over the horizon.

In the entire day I never sailed much over two knots, usually much less, or did not move at all, and so made probably only ten or twelve miles in twenty-four hours—that is, twelve miles east. At the same time I was drifting south in the two-knot current, going faster on current than I did on wind, and in the wrong direction.

That day I ate a can of sardines on two pieces of dried-out bread, a sandwich tasting heavily of salt water.

On this fourth day I began to search the boat for solutions, things that might help me. Strangely, I was not afraid—I think my intimacy with the sea had kicked in and precluded any actual fear—but as Ernest K. Gann wrote in one of his books, certain glands had begun to function well. I found myself breathing deeply for no real reason, sweating a little when it was really quite cool and paying too much attention to loud thumps or splashes against the hull.

I was beginning to understand the concept of time and distance, and the food supply concerned me. I didn't know where I was, but if the wind didn't blow it didn't make any difference how far or not far I was from the coast; if I didn't get back I would get very, very hungry. (I did not think of starving, but the idea was there just the same.)

Except for the dwindling cans of spaghetti, there was no further food on the boat, not in any of the compartments, but the previous owner had left a small tackle box with some lures and little hooks.

The ocean was full of fish.

I would eat.

I really thought it was that simple.

So I put a little feathered lure on a coil of line and hung it over the stern and dragged it well in back of the boat and thought I would have a fish soon. At first I even held the line, waiting for the strike or bite. When it did not come in ten minutes I tied the line off to a cleat and turned back to sailing the boat.

On the morning of the fifth day the wind came

out of the northwest and filled the main and jib. It was blowing at ten or twelve knots—perfect strength for the size of the boat and sail area—and I let them fill and for the first time began to really try to learn to sail.

If I pointed the boat too much into the wind it slowed down. If I pointed it too far off the wind I was going the wrong way and could not make it head east, so I found a compromise and soon had the boat moving east at four and five knots.

It was a major victory. I had wind, the boat was moving and I smiled as I calculated that I would be making more than a hundred miles that day and would undoubtedly be home sometime the next morning.

Of course, I did not know how far I had come. I had also forgotten about sleeping.

The day clipped by and I thought of eating some of my dwindling stock of food, but a cautionary thought held me back. The sailing was still glorious and I drank hot coffee and then cool water from the boat tank and let the rush of the water past the hull convince me of my speed and lack of problems.

Until dark.

There was now a rough half moon and no

clouds so the sky gave light and for a time that fifth night it was glorious. It was sailing as it is meant to be. The boat seemed to leap from wave to wave as they came in on her port bow and she shouldered them aside. She was absolutely alive and I steered with my knee on the tiller and leaned over the side and watched the sea rush by and thought I had never lived so well.

For an hour.

Then another, and then two, and then my head started to droop and my eyelids closed and I caught my chin bouncing off my chest, then settling back and jerking up and then settling down and my lids closed and I slept.

Until the boat skewed up into the wind when I didn't steer and the sails slatted and awakened me. I steered for another half hour, but then the cycle repeated and I closed my eyes and slept as hard as I'd ever slept, slept through the boat heading up into the wind, slept through a change in the direction of the wind, slept with my head against the cabin wall until the sun came up and shone in my eyes. I awakened to look at the compass and realized I had been traveling due south for—I hadn't any idea. An hour? All night?

I was stiff. I stood and stretched the aches

away, then heated water on the little Coleman stove for instant coffee and for the first time looked at my position.

The boat had carried me out here, the boat would carry me back. But I had to sail it. Not just sit and look at the sails and let the boat move but actually try and figure out what was happening, try to learn what it meant to sail.

The boat did not have an autopilot or steering vane, but men had sailed alone without such aids. I had not read his book, but I had read about Joshua Slocum and how he had sailed around the world single-handed from 1895 to 1898, long before steering aids were invented.

But how did it work?

I was rested. I'd resolved to eat only every other day unless I caught a fish, so I had plenty of time to study.

I set the sails and sailed east again and found to my pleasure that the wind had clocked around once more and was allowing me to sail to the northeast a bit.

Fine. I set a heading, adjusted the sails to pull as well as they seemed able to pull and then let go of the little tiller.

The boat promptly headed up into the wind. I

grabbed the tiller and pulled her back over a bit, held her on the right course and found a scrap of line and tied the tiller in place.

And she steered the course.

Not long. She held for seven or eight minutes, then slowly took the wind and headed up again.

I returned her to course, adjusted the tiller a bit and tied it down again. This time she held long enough for me to sip coffee, go to the bathroom, adjust the fishing line and settle back into the cockpit before she crawled up into the wind again. Perhaps ten or twelve minutes and no matter how much I fiddled with the tiller she wouldn't steer longer.

I about gave it up, and then I looked up and for the first time truly realized I was in a sailboat. A *sail*boat. The sails work with the wind against the force of the water to push the boat.

And the sails could be adjusted as well as the tiller. I kept the tiller lashed in one place and started by tuning the jib, the front sail. When I pulled it tighter the boat actually fell off, or tried to go downwind, and when I let it out a bit she pointed back up into the wind, and when I tightened and loosened the mainsail it had the opposite effect. But when I tuned both of them until the boat balanced she practically steered herself.

By experimenting and working at it I finally found a sweet spot where the wind and sails and boat all worked together to hold the course I wanted, and it would hold for hours at a time unless the wind changed direction or died or a large wave came along to slap her out of position.

That discovery would allow me to sleep a bit at night. And on that sixth day I saw another boat.

It was several miles away and looked to be a fishing boat of some kind, perhaps a trawler heading out from San Diego, and while it never answered my frantic waves and kept heading off to the west until it disappeared over the horizon, at least it was another soul and I knew it had come from someplace and was going someplace. And though I did not see another boat that day, I didn't feel so alone. (It is strange that something I thought I did not like then, solitude, would be something I would come to crave many years later.)

I sailed that day and did not eat. I kept track of my direction and speed per hour by writing my compass headings and knots on a piece of notebook paper that I had dried out in the cockpit. I calculated that after twelve hours I had gone nearly sixty miles east with a little north in it. I didn't know about the southerly current yet and how it would pull me off the north heading, so that ultimately I went almost due east.

For now I was doing something, and if it hadn't been for the lack of food I would have been thoroughly enjoying myself. I was definitely starting to feel the extreme hunger and had daydreams and night dreams about food: great Thanksgiving meals, and venison steaks from deer I had killed, and hamburgers with chocolate malts. Then I had several dreams of a time in the army when I was alone at a machine-gun outpost during a training exercise in the winter and somehow I'd been forgotten by the officer in charge and was not fed for two days. At the end of that time a truck came by and I asked the soldier driving if he had any food. He gave me a small box of frosted flakes and a can of grape soda, and I poured the soda on the cereal and ate it with my fingers and have never tasted food so good.

I thought of the frosted flakes and grape pop and actually missed them, and that night, the sixth night, I could stand it no longer and ate half a can of spaghetti and meatballs.

I guess my stomach had shrunk because it completely filled me and I sat dozing half the night, letting the balanced boat steer itself for hours at a time until it would wander off course and I would awaken and realign it. Just before dawn I was leaning over the side to check the fishing line (I never could believe that I could not catch anything) and had my face close to the water in the moonlight when a huge shark hit the side of the boat. I did not know much about sharks then, but I'd seen that shark attack next to the troopship. When this ten-foot shark struck at the moonlight on the side of the boat right in front of my face I thought my heart would stop with fear.

For half a beat I did nothing and then, after the shark was gone, I slammed back across the cockpit so hard I nearly threw myself out of the boat. I never saw the phenomenon again, nor have I heard of it, although a group of killer whales once got very curious about me in a boat and rose up around me and seemed to look down and study me before swimming off.

This shark terrified me for years afterward. This fear, especially coupled with an imagination driven by sleep deprivation, made me afraid to go near the edge of a boat in the dark. Some years later, in a flat calm sea, I slipped over the side alone in the dark and hung there, looking down into the black void with a diving mask on, trying to deal with the fear. I didn't do this long and my imagination ran wild, seeing large and terrible things coming up out of the darkness to eat me, but I lasted several minutes before climbing gratefully back into the boat. I don't think it helped me much because I still don't like to hang in the open ocean in the dark, and as an old army sergeant once described his approach to combat, "Every chance I get, I don't do it."

The next morning I set the tiller and the sails and balanced the boat and went below to make coffee and eat the rest of the spaghetti, which I thought might spoil since I had no refrigeration. I also had to use the head, which was a small seat under a cushion at the front of the boat, and I was sitting there, busy, contemplating, when I heard a woman's voice ask in a perfect English accent, "I say, is anybody aboard the boat?"

I thought I was dreaming or had gone insane. So I did not do anything.

"Hello, the boat—is anybody there?"

It was real!

I stood suddenly, smacking my head on the four-foot overhang, fell back; then, jerking my pants up, I stumbled through the boat to the

companionway and out into the bright sunshine to
see a small wooden sailboat floating nearby, its
nose into the wind and the main pulled over ex-
pertly into a hove-to position. There was an older,
rather squat woman in the cockpit. She had gray
hair with bangs and was wearing a hooded foul-
weather jacket.

"I'm Melanie," she said. "Are you all right?"

For a second I couldn't say anything. I couldn't
see how she could be there and some part of my
brain would not accept it. I shook my head and
tried to think of something to say and when it finally came out all I could find was, "Hello. Would
you like some spaghetti and meatballs?"

The Blue Desert   6

Now it is years and several boats later and I am sitting in La Paz, Mexico, in the Sea of Cortez between the mainland of Mexico and the Baja peninsula. I'm waiting for the northers to subside so that I can ride a force called the Corumel wind and take my catamaran, *Ariel*, further north into the Sea of Cortez and discover some of the sea and, more important, discover more of myself.

Melanie started the process that day. She told me where I was and gave me food and sailed near me for a day and told me more about balancing the boat. She showed me how to really use the sails. I left her and made my way back up the coast to Ventura.

And now as I sit here in La Paz, thinking of my maiden voyage, I know that my life on boats has been about this: not the sailing or the sea so much as learning about self. And almost every boat I have had has taught me something.

My second was an awful sailboat built by a power-boat company, the only vessel I could afford at the time. I tried to make it do until one day, sailing back from Santa Cruz, an island off the California coast, I hit two basking sharks, which tore the rudder off and left a large hole in the stern. This ultimately meant the end of the boat, which wasn't worth fixing.

And then I took about ten years off from sailing while I fell in love with sled dogs. All that time away from the sea it was always in the back of my mind. And one day my heart blew on me, and I couldn't run dogs any longer.

Then, finally, there was only the sea. I took on an old boat, a Hans Christian that needed lots of work but was a good sea boat. She was very, very slow but sure and steady in foul weather. I fixed her up and wanted to do a passage across to the

South Pacific because it is there the sea calls to me most somehow.

But I had books to write.

Instead I took her down Baja and did southern Mexico for a year and a half, plodding at five knots, always five knots, five knots downwind, five knots upwind, five knots surfing down a wave, five knots even falling off a cliff—although I did not get her up into the Sea of Cortez and only saw the ocean from Puerto Vallarta south.

Then the North called again and I took her up the West Coast, slamming into huge seas and some stout wind for days and then weeks until we pulled into the Strait of Juan de Fuca and over to the Inside Passage and worked our way north to Alaska, north to Juneau through beauty that literally cannot be imagined, has to be seen, has to be lived, or you will simply not be complete.

We sat there anchored in the always-daylight while humpback whales fed around the boat, so close they could be touched, turning gently so that their flukes would not hit the boat, missing by inches, with killer whales mugging and fighting and playing around the boat in the clear, cold water, the humpbacks never . . . quite . . .

hitting the boat but always coming close and closer.

Then we sailed back down the West Coast. There we found that the sea gods, as always, are perverse. The wind and seas had reversed and we had to buck the huge waves now coming out of the south. As we sailed I always had the feeling that the sea is not right unless it is crossed; sailing is not enough without a passage.

Then came the cat—the catamaran. She was for sale in Ventura, looking fast and wild even when she sat at the brokerage dock, looking as if she could do all the South Pacific in a week, like a cross between a rocket ship and a boat. I couldn't afford her, and I knew all the stories about catamarans: "They flip, you know," all the wannabe dock sailors told me. "They're not safe, you know, they flip. . . ."

As if my whole life up to that time had somehow been safe and now I would ruin all that because, you know, catamarans flip over.

Well, that's true. If you do things wrong they flip over and there you are. But on the upside, they don't sink, as do keeled boats, because they do not have ballast and the hulls are made of foam that floats. If they flip you wind up with an enormous, really stable life raft, so in the end it's still all a compromise and you give on one side to gain on the other.

But the truth was, the arguments didn't matter. You would have had to shoot me in the head to keep me from the cat. The boat called to me; sitting there, it screamed to me, as a boat must or you will never buy it and never know the sea. I sold the boat I had and I bought the cat. I pulled the mainsail up and unrolled the furled jib and felt the boat surge just as I'd once felt the wind take the first boat I ever sailed on the sea.

Lord, she jumped out, seemed to leap forward with me. The boat I'd just sold made five knots; the cat started there and soon was at ten, then twelve and finally fourteen screaming knots, jumping from wave to wave, flat and fast and leaving little rooster tails in back of her two hulls like a speed boat.

She is a Crowther design, forty-three feet long, twenty-six feet wide, built by a yard in Sydney, Australia, a proper blue-water cat, a sea cat, and nothing about her allowed me to go back to the way I had been, just as a good lead dog once changed my life forever. She has taken me to Hawaii and the miracle of the northeast trade

winds, and then down to Samoa and the southeast
trade winds, and then Tonga and over to Fiji. She
has taken me riding the great South Pacific swells
at twelve knots, and taken me sliding through
moonlight in my shorts and sleeping on the tram-
polines between the hulls while the moon shines
on and through the waves. On the cat I have
watched the dolphins as they leap in silver. And
now, she takes me back to Mexico to show me the
coast of Baja again and then the Sea of Cortez.

To show me the sea. To show me myself. And
never, ever to look back.

Of course, it didn't happen that smoothly.
Nothing ever does.

It has been a long and strange and wonderful
trip, a long and strange and wonderful life in this
boat—California, where I bought her, to Hawaii, to
Samoa, to Tonga, where I tore the rudders off on a
reef, to Fiji, back up to Hawaii, back to California,
down Baja and up into the Sea of Cortez. But for
now . . .

Now it is just before dawn and a soon-to-be
hot sun is appearing in back of a range of high
peaks that look for all the world like jagged bro-

ken teeth. The lagoon is called Balhambra. It's not a completely secure anchorage because it is slightly open to the northwest, where the wind sometimes comes in. But it would be hard to find a place more idyllic. The water is a gentle blue-green with wraparound white sand beaches and stone cliffs that come straight down into the sea.

Small bait fish have congregated around the cat at anchor, trying to hide in her shadow from predators, but it is no use. All around the boat, above and below the water, there is carnage, pure slaughter. Dolphins are feeding, slapping the water with their tails to stun the fish before gobbling them up, and should the dolphins miss any, the pelicans have arrived and are diving to take any fish still alive.

Some of the bait fish try to escape the water, swim up into the air, fly. These are not the flying fish in the Pacific that actually fly, flapping their fins to stay airborne while they dodge predators; these are normal, small fish, terrified, trying to leave their environment, trying to live—and dying in hundreds, thousands, on this beautiful early-summer morning.

The kettle on the propane stove in the galley begins to squeal now. The galley is between the two hulls, the "amahs," as the Polynesians call them, and I go below to make the first cup of tea for the day. Another boat came in the previous afternoon and I scored four Double Stuf Oreo cookies from the crew. I'll have two of them this morning with my tea.

There are morning rituals to perform. Clean the boat, drink tea, sit and think, listen to the shortwave for the weather, where I find Guam is being hit by a typhoon with a staggering, measured 240-knot wind. Though I am many thousands of miles away in a beautiful, calm anchorage, I feel something cold on the back of my neck when I think of what such a wind and the attendant seas would do to my boat, and my life. Shattered bits of both scattered across the water.

I turn on the water maker to change seawater into fresh. The cat—and it is strange that I still think of her thus not as "she," as with other boats, and only rarely by her name, *Ariel*—has taught me many things about technical sailing, but the most important thing to know about sailing a catamaran is that weight is bad. Consequently, she has only two small water tanks, thirty gallons in each hull, and they seem to empty inordinately fast. The water maker is good but slow—a wheezing gallon an hour—but there is plenty of power from three solar panels I installed on the roof of the hard dodger. And seawater, of course, is endless.

Rituals again: I carefully split one Oreo cookie, lick off the filling, then dip each half in the hot tea and eat them soft, almost disintegrating. Delicious and distinctly forbidden because I have heart disease and am supposed to live on a fat-free diet. But I am sixty now, and I can't imagine that I'll die from eating an Oreo cookie since I didn't die from all the crazy dangerous things I've done.

Of course, the sea has tried to kill me on several occasions, has timed itself to coincide with my stupidity and put an end to me. Here in this beautiful lagoon, with time to think of things, and with serenity, some of the madness comes back to me now as I attempt the death-defying feat of eating a second Oreo with my tea.

I remember when I lost control and did not own myself.

Humbled 7

As I said, I once owned a Hans Christian, a boat with a wonderful reputation—at least from word of mouth. She was a thirty-eight-foot, cutter-rigged sloop with a full, deep keel and a pooched-up canoe stern. Her name was *Felicity*.

She was supposed to be a weatherly boat, a tough boat in bad weather. But she was also supposed to be a good sailing boat and be well built. Well, she was slow and cranky and pointed like a hog on ice, and you could have a picnic in the time it took her to come about.

Part of the problem was that she was twenty years old when I bought her and in need of major repairs, and part of it was poor hull design and shoddy workmanship done by a boatyard in China. (I have never bought another Chinese-built boat.) But she was my third boat and I loved her and she was the first boat I took a passage on, and the first boat I hit bad weather on.

There comes a point in owning—or more accurately, being owned by a boat—when it is necessary to *go*. This is more than a beckoning, more than a simple call; it's an order, and if the order is not obeyed there's no sense having a boat. Melville termed it the November in a man's soul that drives him to the sea, and Sterling Hayden, whom I met briefly many years ago in Sausalito, told me that you really had no choice: If the sea called, you went.

So it was with me and *Felicity*. I worked on her for seven months. I put in new rigging and sails, sanded and repaired the blistered fiberglass hull, tried to repair a badly designed motor, gave up and replaced it—it seemed endless. Finally, foolishly, when I was completely sick of working on the boat and sick of boatyards and boatpeople and marinas, I left.

The boat and I were woefully unprepared. The battery boxes were tied in place rather than bolted, which meant that acid could eat through the ropes.

And though there were new sails and rigging, I had not used them. All sail handling had to be done up at the mast—none of the lines were brought back to be controlled from the relative safety of the cockpit—and the boat wiring was a mess.

But one morning I filled the boat with fresh water and some canned goods and aimed her out of the harbor. I headed south from southern California down the coast of Baja.

The sea is sometimes a mysterious place, and much misunderstood. Some time ago there was a nonfiction book and a movie out about a storm in the Atlantic that killed some people. The story is competently written, but the book and the film, with its special effects, threaten to do for boating what *Jaws* did for swimming. Perhaps that's a good thing because it will keep unprepared people from going out there, but the book focuses on one brief period when a disaster hits and doesn't show that for countless other days and weeks the ocean is benign.

The biggest problem in sailing is that there is usually not enough wind, not too much. Much more likely are disasters caused by collision, faulty equipment or fire on board.

And the lack of wind hit me now. I wallowed down the coast using the engine, realizing that my "sail" boat needed nearly a gale to get it moving. We drifted and I ate beans and thought of myself as pretty much the sailorman until we were about halfway down Baja, near a large island named Cedros.

Then it all came at once, without warning.

Squall upon squall, with fifty- and sixty-knot gusts of wind that knocked the boat down one way, then another, building large confused waves that would come over the stern, then sweep the boat from the side, then the bow, then the side, then the stern again—a roar of water and noise and cracks of thunder and bright light as lightning slashed the water all around the boat like incoming artillery. The bolts tore the water, exploded it into steam so that a geyser shot into the air higher than the mast.

I tried to ignore the lightning but I could not forget the story I'd heard of the boat on the way from San Diego to Hawaii with four people aboard, the boat that got hit by lightning, which struck the aluminum mast and traveled down the stainless steel rigging to the inside of the boat, where it slashed back and forth, striking all four people with secondary bursts of energy. Three of them were killed outright and the fourth, injured, man had to sail the boat more than a thousand miles to Hawaii while dealing with three bodies that had once been his close friends and were now fast decomposing. The radio had been knocked out in the storm, but the story is that at last the man got the radio working and the Coast Guard came out with a helicopter to recover the bodies. The Coast Guard takes a dim view of dumping bodies because there have been several instances of men "losing" their wives off the stern in the night. One man "lost" three wives in this way before the authorities got wise and investigated him for murder.

I could not stop thinking about the Hawaiian boat as the bolts struck the water around me, so close that I could smell the ozone. To this day, I can't understand why the lightning did not hit the boat. I had absolutely no control of the situation and in the end all I could do was sit and let the boat be slammed around by the wind and waves and try not to touch anything metal—a completely passive approach to staying alive. The boat did

fine. Because the wind was so around-the-clock,
even though it came in mighty bursts the waves
did not get big enough to endanger the boat.

That would come a year later, when I was sailing from Mexico to California.

I hit weather then that makes me shudder still.
We look back on things and try to find sense in
them by remembering exactly how they came
about.

One morning in March I headed north from
San Diego on *Felicity,* singlehanded, off to a late
start because I'd waited to buy some oil for my engine. There was almost no wind but the barometer
was dropping.

It was the first warning. The barometer almost
never drops significantly in southern California. I
ignored it, thinking it was a small front moving
through.

It was seventy-five miles up to Catalina and
then another seventy-five to Ventura, where I was
going to work on my boat, getting it ready for a
passage to Hawaii. I was actually looking forward
to the overnight run north.

Usually on that particular run if you're single-
handing you stop in Catalina. But I had spent

many nights alone running dogs and was used to not sleeping for a night or two. At night on the sea the sound of the waves comes alive and their whitecaps show in the dark. I enjoyed this kind of sailing. So I decided to keep going all night and get to Ventura just after dawn.

Since I was a little late getting started it was evening when I got to the southeast end of Catalina and came upon the second and third warnings.

For one thing, the sea was literally covered with birds. Gulls and others I didn't recognize rafted up, great shoals of birds covering the water and moving away as I cut through them, heading north. I had never seen so many in one place and marveled at the sight, but I didn't really *see* them, didn't wonder why they should be there. The birds knew there was a storm coming. Because they do no better in bad winds than a boat does—in some cases, worse—they were rafting up in the lee of Catalina to avoid the storm.

And I sailed right through them and didn't question it.

Then there were the cruise ships. Two of them, nestled in the middle of the sea of birds, were also snuggled in the lee of the island. I actually sailed between the two ships and waved at them and kept going.

In my defense, I didn't have a weather fax on the boat. I'd been listening to the radio, which said there was a ". . . weak low moving into the area that would be dissipated by a strong high-pressure system just to the north." The cruise ships had weather faxes and knew a whole lot more than I did.

My own prediction, based on the VHF radio forecast, was that the wind might go up to fifteen or twenty knots, out of the west, but since I was working north with only a little west it would mean a tack for me, and the boat I was on, the Hans Christian, didn't really get to sailing until it had fifteen or twenty knots of wind to drive it.

But the birds knew. They always know. If they didn't, there wouldn't be any birds. And the cruise ships knew. Something big was coming, something big and very, very bad.

I sailed blissfully up alongside Catalina Island, into the coming darkness. I turned on my running lights, sheeted the sails in a bit tighter and motor sailed. The wind had picked up a bit but I was moving in the lee of the island and most of what I was feeling was the dregs of what bled around the north end of the island and trickled south. The wind was straight out of the west and the island, twenty-five or so miles long, is made up of high hills and bluffs that stopped the wind and forced it to go over the top. I was so close in, less than half a mile offshore, that the wind also went over the top of me, and it was so cloudy and deep dark that except for an occasional light gust I had no idea there was much wind at all.

My radio for communications and weather reporting was down at the navigation station, a table inside the boat, and with the engine running I couldn't hear it. Under sail I could hear it well enough, and motoring under normal circumstances I would have gone down inside the boat to listen to the weather.

But this night there was a truly amazing number of boats going back and forth, and I was too afraid of a collision to leave the boat on autopilot long enough to listen to the radio.

So I worked my way north/northwest at five knots until I began to approach the north end of the island. It was extremely dark—even the whitecaps didn't show very well—but at last I began to understand that something was amiss. I became aware of a constant roaring sound. At first I thought it was something wrong with the motor. But it was too loud.

Finally I acknowledged that it was the wind. By now the roar was loud enough to be heard over the sound of the engine. But the sea was not alarming; it was almost flat, with no waves and no real swell, because I was tucked well into the lee of Catalina, almost in the kelp line.

Still, I felt it was time to be cautious and I decided I would put the boat on autopilot, go up and throw a couple of reefs in the main, roll up the jib completely and deploy the much smaller staysail, and then see if I could turn the radio loud enough so that I could hear some of the weather channel over the sound of the wind and engine without leaving the cockpit.

It was very nearly the last time I ever sailed a boat.

All this time I had been working north at five knots and was approaching the end of the island. As I rolled up the jib with the lines from the cockpit I could see the north-end light ahead. I counted the flashes and timed them and knew from their position on the chart that I would soon be out of the lee. I had a harness and safety line on and I clipped the line into the jackstay that went forward and moved up to the mast to reef.

I was halfway there when we got hit.

With me halfway to the mast, the whole world went mad.

The wind hit the boat with a demonic shriek, screaming, roaring, driving spray into my eyes and blinding me. I felt the boat go over on her beam and slide sideways. I was thrown off the boat, hanging in my lifeline and harness on the down side, dangling across the deck and in the water, disoriented, upside down, then right side up, the wind a wild howling filling my ears, my mind, my soul, and with the sudden onslaught of wind came the waves.

They were true monsters, steepsided, galloping, twenty, thirty feet high, almost vertical walls with breaking tops that caught the boat and held her down on her side with me in the water, clawing to get back on, ripping my nails, cutting my hands, now fighting to live, not sail, not obey the call of the sea, nothing noble or high-flown now but just to live, get on the boat and *live*. Even while I fought I remembered the tales of boats found sailing on their own with their owners, singlehanders, hanging off the stern dead in their harnesses because they couldn't get back on the boat before hypothermia stopped their ability to function and they drowned.

What saved me was the mainsail. I'd bought a new one, but frugality had reared its penny-pinching head and I had decided to use the old mainsail until it was completely shot before putting the new one on. The sail was twenty years old and the sun and wind had done their work on the threads and with a stunning *whaaaack!* the stitching let go and the sail exploded downwind. With the sail in tatters the boat's ten-thousand-pound lead keel could work and it pulled her momentarily upright between the slamming waves. I was unceremoniously jerked back over the side and lay sprawled on the cabin top, dripping and cold, my clothing soaked under the foul-weather gear. But I was up and out of the water. I was clutching at anything and everything like a crab, slithering back toward the cockpit, still half blinded by spray—and it's difficult to believe what salt water driven into your eyes at high velocity can feel like until it happens to you; the pain is immediate, excruciating and constant—I was little more than an animal, but I was up, and out of the water.

The boat slammed down again, but by this time

I had reached the temporary protection of the cockpit—temporary because the next wave broke quartering over the stern and filled the cockpit with seawater, perhaps a thousand pounds of it, which almost dragged her back under by the stern. I thought I actually felt her sinking but the next wave rolled her again and dumped the water out.

She seemed to be foundering, staggering, and I grabbed the wheel. Maybe I could somehow help her by steering. I'd read of boats in storms running downwind and kept from being knocked over and down by being cautiously steered between the peaks, in the "valleys" of the waves, but there is a world of difference between sitting of a quiet evening reading about storm tactics and trying to do them when the wind is tearing you apart, the seas are slamming you and the spray has you virtually blind. I couldn't even see the waves, let alone find a peak or a valley, and the concept of steering becomes meaningless when you are spending more time hanging off the side of the wheel than standing up to it.

There was never a time when it abated. Not a moment when I could shrug and shake and take a breather or catch up or even react sanely to what was happening. The boat slammed and

pounded and rolled and shuddered and the cockpit filled and she would seem to be foundering
and then she would roll and empty—the three
little inch-and-a-half cockpit drains were a joke;
the boat would take on two or three hundred gallons and turn the large cockpit into a full-size
Jacuzzi. I was under water more than I was out of
it. I had closed the companionway, but hundreds
of gallons went down into the boat and I could
hear the twelve-volt bilge pump working to get rid
of the water, putting out a little half-inch stream
while gallons poured in through the louvered
doors of the companionway. Thank God the motor
kept running; it could do nothing to move the boat
in such waves but it kept the electrical system from
running down, so the bilge pump kept working.

And then it was over.

Just that fast. I was suddenly standing on a boat
that made sense; the rolling and pitching had
stopped and while I could still hear the wind roaring and tearing, it was back past the stern, and the
boat was once again in the lee of the island in
quiet water.

Later I figured what had happened. We had just
barely nosed past the island, only just come out

into the wind-shear line, where we got hit. The wind tore at the bow, smashed it around as it pounded the boat over, completely turning it end over end, and though it was moved sideways the keel caught the water and the wind propelled it forward as well, except that we were now moving in the opposite direction, the boat hull itself acting as a sail to drive her back into the lee. I had nothing to do with it. She went out and came back herself, sail hanging in tatters from the mast and boom.

The motor propelled us peacefully at five-and-a-half knots. The boat moved smoothly, flat in the quiet water along the kelp beds, and I stood, soaked, blasted into a kind of shock, my hand on the wheel in a counterfeit control. I could hear the hum and squirt of the bilge pump and I looked back into the darkness, tried to see what was there, but there was only blackness and the roaring of the wind and the loud smashing hiss of the breaking waves.

I knew that I had been close to death and that only luck had kept me alive and that I would go back down to the other end of the island and take a mooring in the little harbor of Avalon and make a hot breakfast and spend a day and a night sleeping and resting and thanking whatever higher power it was that kept me alive, and I shivered and the motion pulled up the sleeve of my foul-weather jacket and I saw my watch and thought, no, it's broken, this can't be.

The total elapsed time was twenty-two minutes, start to finish. My life was completely changed and I would never look at the sea the same way again.

And only twenty-two minutes had passed.

Later I learned: It was truly a killer storm. Boats were lost, lives were lost. One of the large ferries that went back and forth to the mainland had been hit by a wave so high and strong that it took out the second-floor windows on one side and then went on *through* the boat and tore the windows out the other side as well, from the inside out.

The storm went on through California and Arizona and destroyed buildings and killed people all the way to El Paso, Texas, before it finally broke apart and ended.

I don't know how strong the wind was that hit me because I had no anemometer on my boat. But when I got to Avalon the wind coming over the back and blowing out through the sheltered harbor itself had sporadic gusts up to fifty knots and a man there said there'd been measured gusts north of Catalina Island that went over a hundred knots.

All that day I lay listening to the wind screaming overhead, dozing safely in my bunk, and all I could think was: There are people who have been in storms that lasted many hours, sometimes *days,* in the open sea.

I was nearly killed in twenty-two minutes.

But I was still there, and that very night I began making plans. That night I decided: Someday I would try the one great passage of the sailor's world. Someday I would try to sail around Cape Horn.

About the Author

Gary Paulsen is the distinguished author of many critically acclaimed books for young people, including three Newbery Honor books: *The Winter Room, Hatchet* and *Dogsong*. His novel *The Haymeadow* received the Western Writers of America Golden Spur Award. Among his newest Random House books are *The Glass Café: Or the Stripper and the State; How My Mother Started a War with the System That Made Us Kind of Rich and a Little Bit Famous; How Angel Peterson Got His Name: And Other Outrageous Tales About Extreme Sports; Guts: The True Stories Behind* Hatchet *and the Brian Books; The Beet Fields: Memories of a Sixteenth Summer; Alida's Song* (a companion to *The Cookcamp*); *Soldier's Heart; The Transall Saga; My Life in Dog Years; Sarny: A Life Remembered* (a companion to *Nightjohn*); *Brian's Return* and *Brian's Winter* (companions to *Hatchet*); *Father Water, Mother Woods: Essays on Fishing and Hunting in the North Woods* and five books about Francis Tucket's adventures in the Old West. Gary Paulsen has also published fiction and nonfiction for adults, as well as picture books illustrated by his wife, the painter Ruth Wright Paulsen. Their most recent book is *Canoe Days*. The Paulsens live in New Mexico and on the Pacific Ocean.